THE SAFEST PLACE ON EARTH

**Mark Finley
and Steven Mosley**

Pacific Press® Publishing Association
Nampa, Idaho
Oshawa, Ontario, Canada
www.pacificpress.com

Cover design by Fred Knopper
Cover photos by Palmer Halvorson

Copyright © 2003 by
Pacific Press® Publishing Association
Printed in the United States of America
All Rights Reserved

Additional copies of this book may be purchased at
www.adventistbookcenter.com

All Bible quotations not otherwise credited are from the
New King James Version, © 1979, 1980, 1982 by
Thomas Nelson, Inc. Used by permission.

ISBN: 0-8163-1985-5

03 04 05 06 07 • 5 4 3 2 1

Contents

The Forgotten Boundary

So much is flying past in our lives. So much is going on every day. It's hard to stop the crazy pace. It's hard to recognize boundaries. Sometimes you can't even figure out where *you* leave off and where everything else begins.

You may not know it yet, but God has a suggestion on how you can actually stop the relentless rush of time.

In recent years we've become keenly aware of something called "boundary issues." Some people have a hard time setting boundaries in their lives. Some people have a hard time saying No when they really should.

Take a woman like Rita, for example. She's a single mother trying hard to rear three little boys. She also has some friends from church who are rather demanding. They expect her to organize social events for the singles group. They expect her to lead out in activities. This is her gift, they say, and she ought to be exercising it.

So Rita tries. She badly needs the affirmation of her friends. But she finds herself stretched very thin. Her children require a lot of attention. And there are always so many church events to prepare for. So, Rita's life is getting out of control, but she just can't say No. She thinks it's her duty to always say Yes to her friends.

Or take a man like Mike. He's an insurance salesman who likes to keep everybody happy. He tries to keep his wife happy. He tries to keep people at work happy. And he tries to keep his mother happy. She always seems to need him—even though she's in fairly good health. She needs Mike to fix a leaky faucet or the jammed garbage disposal. She needs Mike to sort out her bills. She needs him to run errands. She needs him around when she's depressed.

Mike's wife wonders why he's gone all the time. She can't understand why her mother-in-law can't do these things for herself. And Mike feels torn. He wants to be a better husband. But how can he say No when his mother calls? That would make him feel like an ungrateful son.

Rita and Mike are classic examples of people who can't set good boundaries. They are constantly bending themselves out of shape—in order to fit into other people's shapes. And so they lose a shape of their own.

They can't seem to keep intrusive, controlling people away. They can't tell people No when they really need to. They can't say, "I'm sorry, but that's an unreasonable expectation." They can't say, "I'm sorry, but I can't fit that into my life right now."

People without boundaries take on too much. They're molded by the expectations of others. And so, they are forever caught up in a rush of trying to do too much and trying to please too many people.

All of us get caught up in that rush in one way or another. In our world today, it's easy to take on too many chores. Everything seems to happen faster and faster.

- The speed of the microchip doubles every eighteen months.
- Two-day express mail used to be fast enough for almost anybody. But now, we have to have overnight deliveries. And even that is "snail mail" according to people hooked on the instant communication of email.
- Even names have to get faster. It took too long to say, "Federal Express," so now those trucks and planes speeding by read, "Fed Ex."

The world keeps going faster. And that makes all the demands placed upon us tougher to deal with. It makes the struggles of people without boundaries even more acute.

How do we put up boundaries in a world in which one day just flows into the next, one week into the next, one year into the next? How do we stop the rush in a way that's meaningful for us?

Well, I'd like to suggest that God Himself has given us a good starting point. He has shown us a very meaningful boundary—a boundary in time. Let's take a look at it. We first find it in the Bible, in the book of Genesis.

In the first few chapters of Genesis we discover that God gave us two important institutions when He created our world. The first was marriage. Our Creator united Adam and Eve as one flesh. He gave them the Garden of Eden as a beautiful home in which to rear their family. The second is described in Genesis, chapter two: "Then God blessed the seventh day and sanctified it, because in it He rested from all His work which God had created and made" (Gen. 2:3).

At the end of the six days of creation week, God instituted the Sabbath. He made the seventh day special and holy. He rested from His work. And this became an example for His people. They, too, were to rest from all their work on the Sabbath.

The Sabbath was a holy boundary placed in the weekly cycle. It stopped the flow of endless time, the endless rush of doing our chores.

The Sabbath is a way to stop. But it means more than just time off from work. The book of Deuteronomy reminds God's people of this forgotten boundary. "Observe the Sabbath day by keeping it holy, as the Lord your God has commanded you" (Deut. 5:12, NIV).

We are commanded to keep this certain day holy. It's a day set apart from all the other days of the week. It's special. It's quality time. It's a time in which we can focus on our most important relationships—

our relationship with God and our relationships with our loved ones.

And yes, it's a time when we can say No to all other demands, all the other things that clutter up our lives. The Sabbath is a boundary that gives us breathing room.

The Sabbath calls us away from our usual routines. And it asks us to make the pursuit of spiritual things a delight. Reading good books, exploring nature, spending quiet time together as a family—these are the things we typically neglect. Why? Because we don't have good boundaries. We let so many other demands fill up our lives.

Now, I want you to understand that this Sabbath idea is unique in the whole history of religion. There are many holy *things* in the religions of the world. People have ascribed holiness to everything from cows to the bones of saints. Men have worshipped idols of every conceivable kind.

And there are many holy *places* in the religions of the world. Hindus travel thousands of miles to bathe in the sacred waters of the Ganges. Moslems make long pilgrimages to the holy city of Mecca. Buddhists revere the site where Buddha experienced enlightenment.

But in the Bible, we find the unique idea of holiness in *time*. God created a holy setting where human beings could be specially blessed. But He did not restrict it to a certain location. We don't have to make long pilgrimages to arrive at God's holy place. No, He has placed His holy setting in time, equally accessible to everyone. It's a quality time for everyone. It's a boundary for everyone.

People without boundaries are carrying too many burdens. They are oppressed by the demands and expectations of others. Well, did you know that deliverance from oppression is one of the things memorialized by the Sabbath, by that Sabbath boundary? God gives us a memorial of deliverance from oppression in the Sabbath. The Sabbath symbolizes deliverance.

We've already seen how the Sabbath calls us back to our Creator, the One who rested on the seventh day of Creation, the One who wants to make us healthy and whole. The Sabbath also calls us back to God as our personal Redeemer.

Listen to how the book of Deuteronomy amplifies the meaning of the Sabbath: "And remember that you were a slave in the land of Egypt, and that the Lord your God brought you out from there by a mighty hand and by an outstretched arm; therefore the Lord your God commanded you to keep the Sabbath day" (Deut. 5:15).

The Sabbath, we find here, is a memorial of God's deliverance. He is the great Rescuer. And whom did He rescue? People who had to work all the time. Slaves in Egypt toiling through the monotonous hours. Slaves with no hope that their endless labor would ever give them freedom. That's whom God rescued. His mighty hand and outstretched arm swept them from under the control of a tyrannical Pharaoh.

There are many "slaves" today who need a similar rescue. Their endless toil serves only to make them less and less free; they have less and less time. Their endless attempts to please everybody make them only more frustrated. Their endless attempts to meet everyone's demands make them only more helpless. And there is no tyrant as merciless as our own desperate fear, our own sense of inadequacy.

We need God the Deliverer today just as much as the Hebrews did back then. We need Him to come in and throw down His Sabbath, His boundary, at the end of our week too.

He says, "Stop! There is only one way to be free. And that's to trust your Creator. Yes, trust Me. Invest your time in a relationship with Me, and I will become your Deliverer."

Thank God for Sabbath rest! It's the answer for our stress-intensive environment. It's a meaningful boundary for us. It tells us there is more to life than just a wearying routine.

You know, people with boundary problems often grew up in homes where the boundaries were blurred. They had to constantly try to please someone in order to be accepted. Perhaps as a child they even had to take care of an addicted or needy parent. They may have learned to take on other people's problems as their own.

In other words, people with boundary problems often have acceptance problems. They keep working so hard in order to be accepted. They can't rest because they never feel quite accepted.

Well, let me tell you what the New Testament has to say about Sabbath rest, and why Sabbath rest is relevant to us as believers.

The Sabbath actually shows us that we can truly rest in Christ. That's right, rest in Christ.

This is what the writer of Hebrews makes clear. In the fourth chapter, he writes about the seventh day; and he writes about what this day of rest really means for believers. This is what he says: "There remains therefore a rest for the people of God. For he who has entered His [God's] rest has himself also ceased from his works as God did from His" (Heb. 4:9, 10).

Entering into Sabbath rest means that we cease from our works; we no longer try to manufacture salvation; we no longer try to be accepted on the basis of our own good works. God has done the work for us in Christ. Christ has completed the work of our redemption.

He did it by the shores of the Sea of Galilee. He did it on the dusty trails of Judea. He did it in the streets of Jerusalem. Jesus Christ lived out a perfect, righteous life in *our* world, in *our* environment. And then He poured out that life on the cross— deliberately, willingly. He gave up His perfect life as a substitute for our sinful life.

In a sense, this Carpenter from Nazareth carved a special dwelling for us out of His righteousness. We can find refuge there; we can be safe there. His work is complete. It is finished. We can confidently rest in the forgiveness that Christ offers.

We can know that, *in Christ,* we are accepted by the heavenly Father.

Sabbath rest is about being accepted by our Father in heaven. Do you see why this can be so meaningful for people without boundaries?

The Sabbath boundary says, "Here is where you can stop; here is where you can rest. You can say No to demanding people because God has said Yes to you. He has said Yes in Jesus Christ. He has given you righteousness in Jesus Christ."

The Sabbath is a meaningful boundary that can stick with us. It can stick with us in a world of constant change and widespread confusion. It can be an island of stability.

Our families really need that today. Our children really need that so much today. All around them, things are falling apart. Traditional values crumble, families are fractured, trust is betrayed. But the Sabbath proclaims that God is constant, His values are unchanging.

Listen to these words of God found in Exodus—words that speak to our hearts with meaning: "You shall surely observe My sabbaths; for this is a sign between Me and you throughout your generations, that you may know that I am the Lord who sanctifies you." (Exod. 31:13, NASB).

The Sabbath is a sign that continues through generation after generation. It points generation after generation toward the Lord, who sanctifies us, who sets us apart. Its observance can mark out a boundary between what is most important and what is not so important. It can help us concentrate on the things that matter most.

A story is told of that terrible time when countless people were sent to Nazi concentration camps. At the train terminal in one of the death camps, the SS officers began separating able-bodied men from the women and children. One father who was sent to the camp was a member of a royal family. He realized with a start that he might never see his young son again. So he knelt down beside the boy and held him by the shoulders. "Michael," he said, "no matter what happens, I want you to always remember one thing. You're special; you're the son of a king!"

Soon father and son were separated by the soldiers. They were marched off to different sections of the camp. The two never saw each other again.

Michael learned much later that his father had perished in a gas chamber. And he had to go out alone and try to make his way in the world. But his father's last words would always stay with him. "You're the son of a king, Michael." And so Michael determined that, whatever came, he would behave like the son of a king.

The Sabbath is an important message from our heavenly Father, a sign that declares: "You are a child of the King of the universe. I claim you as my own."

And it's a sign that we may always carry with us, a reminder of our special identity. You don't have to be pressured into someone else's mold. You don't have to be manipulated into someone else's shape. God is shaping you as His child. God is claiming you as His own. He wants you to know that you, too, are a child of the King.

Do you need to draw a meaningful boundary in your own life today? Do you need to have quality time with your Maker, your Redeemer? Do you need to truly rest in Jesus Christ?

I invite you to make the Sabbath experience a part of your walk with God. I invite you to stop the endless rush of time, the endless demands, the endless chores. I invite you to begin experiencing Sabbath rest.

* * * * *

"Dear Father, Thank You for the gift of the Sabbath. Thank You for caring about our needs from the very beginning of Creation. Thank You for giving us true spiritual rest through Jesus Christ. We want to experience that each week. We want to truly enter Sabbath rest. We want that meaningful boundary in our lives. Thank You for this blessing. Keep us close to You, we pray in the name of the Savior, Jesus Christ, our Lord. Amen."

The Buzz About the Sabbath

For a long time, it was regarded as an exclusively Hebrew practice, something that separated Jews from Gentiles. It was thought of as a part of Old Testament ritual and ceremony. But recently, the Sabbath, this "palace in time," has been popping up in the most secular of places. It's becoming part of the mainstream, a way of coping with the stresses and strains of contemporary life. And now, more and more people of faith are beginning to discover just why it has a special meaning for Christians.

Not long ago, I was looking through the Sunday edition of the *Los Angeles Times* and I came across a special insert. I noticed the entire issue was devoted to "The Buzz About Shabbat."

Evidently, the Sabbath has become something of a hot topic. These people had made quite an investment in telling the million-plus readers of the *Times* about it.

Inside, I found articles from a wide range of thought leaders and celebrities—Larry King and Kirk

Douglas, Michael Medved and Uri Geller, Shimon Peres and Arianna Huffington. And they were all talking about the Sabbath, about what the Sabbath has meant in their personal lives. Why?

Well, what the contributors to this special magazine are saying is this: Human beings desperately need this special day of rest. We need it more than ever. The world is busier and noisier and more intense and more demanding than at any time in history. And the Sabbath can keep us from being consumed by it.

Rabbi David Wolpe writes that we need the Sabbath because "the modern world never whispers." Our cities are like arcades without exits. Urgent voices, flashing signs, and an endless stream of media surround us.

Wolpe notes that the people around him have no time. Their lives are crowded. No time for seeing their friends or playing with their overscheduled children or just sitting quietly by a window. They always have to be driving somewhere or checking their email or returning calls on the telephone or their cell phones or returning an email. We're always taking care of business.

But the Sabbath, Wolpe writes, is a time to stop, to savor the blessings we have, to bless those around us who matter most.

Michael Steinhardt worked as an investor on Wall Street for more than thirty years. He describes the stresses of following the stock market for a living. But he looks back on the Sabbaths spent with his family as a way to keep things in perspective. In fact, he says that if it weren't for this period of rest and reflection, he wouldn't have been able to remain productive.

I'm used to seeing in-depth reports in America's leading newspapers about things such as global warming or presidential scandals or the state of the economy. But all this coverage for something that many people have regarded as a quaint Jewish ritual is really remarkable.

People today are rediscovering the value of the Sabbath. Many Jews are rediscovering it as part of their heritage. When Joseph Lieberman was a vice-presidential candidate, people noticed that he wasn't afraid to talk about his faith. When he talked about core values, he talked about trust in God.

And he could describe what the Sabbath meant to him. That topic, in fact, occupied front-page news across America. Lieberman had to reveal what he would do and would not do on the Sabbath, if he were elected vice president.

The Sabbath has been making something of a comeback. But what's most interesting is that this is not confined to Jewish circles. It's making a come-back in downtown USA, where people are burning out on the everincreasing pace of urban life. It's making a comeback in the suburbs, where families are looking for traditions they can observe that will bind them together.

If you check <amazon.com> today, you'll find hundreds of matches for *Sabbath*. There are a lot of books on the subject. You'll find books such as *Sabbath: Find-*

ing Rest, Renewal, and Delight in Our Busy Lives or *Sabbath Sense: A Spiritual Antidote for the Overworked.*

But here's the most fascinating aspect of the Sabbath comeback. Most recently, it's Christians who are rediscovering God's original day of rest. More and more Christians are exploring what the Sabbath can mean in their own lives as believers.

Interest is so keen that they've started creating their own Web sites. You can visit the "Global Sabbath Network" and find out about those who "worship Jesus Christ as Lord of the Sabbath, and honor the Sabbath of the Lord."

You can log onto "Christian Sabbath Keepers" and check out "Resources for Sabbath Keepers Throughout the World."

You can participate in the "Evangelical Sabbath Fellowship" or exchange messages on the "Spirit-filled Sabbatarian E-mail Conference."

If you walk into a Christian or evangelical bookstore today, you'll find that interest in the Sabbath has joined the Christian mainstream. Don Postema is pastor of Campus Chapel at the University of Michigan. He comes from the Reformed tradition. One of his popular books is *Catch Your Breath: God's Invitation to Sabbath Rest.*

The Banner of Truth trust recently published a book by Walter Chantry with the title *Call the Sabbath a Delight.* Eerdmans Publishing in Grand Rapids, Michigan, recently came out with *Keeping the Sabbath Wholly,* by Marva Dawn. And the Presbyterian and Reformed publishing house just brought us a book by Bruce Ray called *Celebrating the Sabbath—Find Rest in a Restless World.*

Yes, the Sabbath has been making a comeback. Lots of people are talking about it. Lots of Christians are talking about it.

But is this phenomenon really such a good thing? Does Sabbath keeping really fit into the faith of the New Testament? Is it a legitimate part of Christian life, or is it a way back to legalism, back to the tyranny of the law? These are questions many people haven't considered.

Now, I think it's pretty easy to see how the Sabbath as a day of rest can be a blessing. We could all use that rhythm of rest and reflection in our lives. Spending special time with our families, spending special time with God—it's hard to argue against that. After all, the Sabbath was God's gift to humanity back at the beginning, back at Creation.

And may I remind you, there were no Jews around at Creation. According to Jesus, the Sabbath was given to *humankind,* it was given to Adam and Eve, to be kept all through the centuries as a sign of love between God and us.

But what about today? What does the Sabbath mean for the Christian? That's what I'd like us to consider. Can Sabbath keeping be part of faith in Christ, or is it really a denial of grace?

Let's look at what the New Testament has to say.

The apostle Paul is the great champion of grace in the New Testament, the one who lays out what salvation by faith in Christ is all about. He, more than anyone else, made a stand against legalism. He made a stand against those who insisted everybody had to be circumcised to be saved. He made a stand against those who insisted everybody had to observe all the Jewish or Hebrew traditions to be saved. He made a stand against those who insisted everybody had to come to God through the Old Testament system of sacrifices.

In Colossians, chapter two, Paul describes what Jesus accomplished through His death and resurrection. "God made you alive with Christ. He forgave us all our sins, having canceled the written code, with its regulations, that was against us and that stood opposed to us; he took it away, nailing it to the cross." (Col. 2:13, 14, NIV).

Old Testament rituals and regulations, Paul said, were "a shadow of things to come" (verse 17). They pointed forward to Christ. So, when Christ came, that whole system came to an end. It was fulfilled in Christ.

After Christ's death, people could place their faith in what He accomplished. They didn't need to focus on symbols anymore. Symbols aren't the means of salvation. In fact, no religious ritual of any kind is a means of salvation. No amount of doing "the works of the law" can save us. Only Christ's grace can save us.

That's what the apostle Paul makes clear in all his New Testament letters.

So, the question I'd like to ask is this: Is Sabbath keeping a part of that Old Testament system of regulations? Is it part of the "shadow of things to come," which was done away with at the cross? The Sabbath is certainly part of Jewish tradition. Does that mean it can't be part of Christian tradition or Christian practice? In other words, does Sabbath observance take us back to legalism, back to the legalism that Paul warns us about?

Definitely, Paul stated that we are not "under the law" (Gal. 5:18), that is, we don't earn salvation by keeping it. That's what he said we *don't* do. But what *do* we do? How is the Christian supposed to relate to the law? Specifically, how is the Christian supposed to relate to God's *moral* law. We know that the Old Testament sacrificial system with its rules and regulations has been done away with. But what about the law that is supposed to be eternal? What about the Ten Commandments?

In Romans, the apostle Paul makes very plain God's thoughts regarding the law. He says: "For what the law could not do in that it was weak through the flesh, God did by sending His own Son in the likeness of sinful flesh, on account of sin: He condemned sin in the flesh, that the righteous requirement of the law might be fulfilled in us who do not walk according to the flesh but according to the Spirit" (Rom. 8:3, 4).

The law, as a means of salvation, is weak. The law, as a means of transformation, is weak. It's weak because of our own sinful nature. It's weak because of the fallen nature of our own hearts. The law can't pull us up to meet its requirements. But Jesus did meet those requirements. He fulfilled the law on our behalf. That's how He saves us. That's how He justifies us.

And furthermore, Christ's Spirit inside of us can help us grow. The Spirit can help us begin fulfilling "the righteous requirements of the law" in our own lives.

Here is something we all need to understand. The law fails as a *means* of getting us to God. But once we're accepted by God, the law is a legitimate *end*. It's a legitimate objective. We can aim at incorporating God's moral principles into our lives—not in order to be saved, but because we *are* saved, not in order to be loved by God, but because we *are* loved.

Think back to when you were growing up. Did your mom or dad ever stand you against the wall, shoulders back, chin out, and put a ruler on the top of your head?

Remember that? They'd make a little line with a pencil. "That's how tall you are," they said. "Look at that! Look how much you've grown!"

And a few months later, they'd stand you in the same spot and make another little line. "My, look at how much you've grown!"

Now, normal parents do that just so their kids can see they're making progress. Nobody imagines that measuring kids actually makes them grow. No one thinks that if they just measured their child a little more often, he or she would have a growth spurt.

God's moral law is a ruler that measures us. It shows us how we're making progress in terms of God's standards, how we are growing spiritually by His grace. But it can't *make* us grow. It fails as a *means* of transformation.

But it's an excellent *end,* an excellent objective.

I was visiting an elementary school and noticed a life-size poster of Michael Jordan there; it was taped on a classroom door. And the poster was marked off vertically in feet and inches—all the way up to Jordan's six-foot-six.

There were names of first and second graders scrawled on that poster, around the basketball player's knees. That's where they'd all lined up and been measured.

Now that teacher wasn't scolding anyone for being so much shorter than Michael Jordan. That teacher wasn't trying to intimidate anyone into growing taller. But those kids loved comparing themselves to their basketball hero. They were making some progress. Someday, just maybe, they'd be way up there with Air Jordan.

God's moral law is something we can look up to and measure ourselves against. It isn't the *means* of growth. But it's a legitimate *end*. Those are "righteous requirements" that we're looking up to.

So now, back to our central question. What about the Sabbath? Is Sabbath keeping part of the "righteous requirements of the law"?

Well, what do we find in the Ten Commandments? Let's look at Exodus, chapter 20. We find the Sabbath deeply embedded in the heart of God's moral law. The fourth commandment says: "Remember the Sabbath day, to keep it holy. Six days you shall labor and do all your work, but the seventh day is the Sabbath of the Lord your God" (Exod. 20:8-10).

"Remember the Sabbath day." There it is, right along with "You shall not murder," right along with "You shall not commit adultery." It certainly sounds as if it's part of God's moral law. It certainly sounds like a "righteous requirement." After all, you don't hear Christians saying it's OK to kill or commit adultery because now we're "not under the law, but under grace."

But what about the New Testament? Is this Sabbath commandment given legitimacy by the Gospel writers? Is it part of the "substance" that belongs to Christ, or just a "shadow of things to come"?

Well, how about if we look at Jesus Himself. How did Jesus relate to this Sabbath commandment?

Jesus actually spent a great deal of His time trying to rehabilitate the Sabbath. The Pharisees and Sadducees had made it a burdensome obligation. They'd loaded down the Sabbath with all kinds of regulations. Jesus wanted it to be a day of healing and blessing. He had many conflicts with Jewish leaders over this issue.

And during one such conflict, this is what He said, "The Sabbath was made for man, and not man for the Sabbath. Therefore the Son of Man is also Lord of the Sabbath" (Mark 2:27, 28).

Jesus' contemporaries were trying to stuff human beings into their small-minded religion, trying to make everyone conform to their petty Sabbath regulations. But Jesus reminded them that the Sabbath was made for men and women. It was given to us at Creation—for our benefit.

And furthermore, Jesus identified Himself as "Lord of the Sabbath." Now think about that. I don't think Jesus would have said that if He were trying to do away with the Sabbath.

Challenging the Pharisees' ideas about Sabbath observance occupied a lot of Jesus' time. It would have been much easier for Him to simply say, "The Sabbath is irrelevant." Instead, He said, "The Sabbath was made for man, for human beings."

I'd like to return to that elementary-school classroom and to that Michael Jordan poster. During recess, you could watch the first and second graders playing with a plastic basketball stand. It stood about four feet off the ground. Several of the boys were really getting into it. They'd bounce a little rubber ball around as best they could. They'd take wild shots and celebrate if they hit the backboard.

Some of the bigger boys would even try to jump in the air and stuff the ball. They usually fumbled it away in the process. But in their imaginations they were sailing toward the hoop just like Air Jordan.

Sometimes those kids didn't want to stop playing to eat their lunch. But all the teacher had to do was mention something about how athletes train. Yes, athletes such as Michael Jordan go through a long period of training. They have to exercise. They have to make sure they eat healthful food.

Well, immediately the kids would gobble up their lunch and down their cartons of milk. There wasn't a single first or second grader who said, "Yeah, maybe Michael Jordan needs to do that, but I don't."

No kid assumes he's beyond that. Of course they don't. They're looking up at that big, glorious poster. They want to be like Mike.

What about Christians? We all want to be like Jesus, right? He's the fulfillment of the law. He's the One we're following.

Well, listen to what Luke tells us about Jesus' practice. If Jesus is somebody whom we admire, somebody we want to be like, then listen to this: "And as His [Jesus'] custom was, He went into the synagogue on the Sabbath day" (Luke 4:16).

The synagogue, of course, was the church. Jesus observed the Sabbath. It was part of His spiritual discipline. It was part of His relationship with the Father.

But when it comes to our Sabbath observance, many of us are saying, in effect, "I'm beyond that. Maybe Jesus needed to do that for some reason, but I don't."

Well, I'm sorry, but nobody I know is more spiritually mature than Jesus. Nobody I know is on some higher spiritual plane than Jesus. If He needed it, we need it. I need it, and you need it. If Jesus worked hard to recover the Sabbath as a day of blessing, then we need to take advantage of it as well.

Let me show you one more New Testament passage about the Sabbath—one that clearly connects it to grace. The book of Hebrews relates Sabbath rest to the rest of faith. In chapter four, the author reminds his readers of the moment at Creation when God "rested on the seventh day from all His works." And then he says: "There remains therefore a rest for the people of God. For he who has entered His rest has himself also ceased from his works as God did from His" (Heb. 4:9, 10).

Why is this rest still legitimate "for the people of God"? Because it embodies our rest in Christ. Those who aren't trying to work their way to heaven, those who aren't relying on "the works of the law," can rest in the finished work of Christ. They can rest in faith because He has fulfilled the law on their behalf.

The Sabbath serves today as a wonderful symbol of our trust in Christ. It's a part of the life of faith, the life of grace. I believe that it has a legitimate place in Christian tradition, in Christian faith, and in Christian practice.

Kirk Douglas shares a memory of his mother that has stuck with him through the decades. She was in a hospital, dying of pneumonia. Kirk and his sisters gathered around her bed to keep a vigil. On Friday, at dusk, his mother roused herself and said, "Don't forget to light the Sabbath candles."

Well, they started to light four candles there in the room, but nurses rushed in screaming. With all that oxygen in the room, they could have blown up the whole hospital!

Kirk was feeling scared as he stared at his mother. He'd seen a look of terror in the eyes of other loved ones who'd passed away. But now he noticed something different. He said, "She looked up at me and smiled a clear, serene smile. It was the kind of smile she used to have on her face every Sabbath when she sat on the porch with her prayer book."

Here was a woman who was resting in God. A phrase from a religious text came to Kirk's mind: "Dying by the kiss of God."

The Sabbath is a reminder that we can all rest in God. It's a reminder to Christians that we can rest in Christ. We can live by the kiss of God. We can live by grace, live by faith.

Have you discovered the rest that only Christ can bring? Have you discovered the peace that only a relationship with Him can create? Why not start by devoting each Sabbath to Him? Make it a meaningful time of rest and reflection. Use it to strengthen your faith. Use it to let God's grace sink in. You don't have to work for it. You don't have to earn it. Just accept it. Just rest.

Every Sabbath, come apart and say, "Dear Lord, thank You for creating me. Life is a gift, and I acknowledge it to you this Sabbath."

Every Sabbath come apart and say, "Lord, thank You for redeeming me. Salvation is a gift, and this Sabbath I acknowledge it by resting in You."

Why not, right now, make a decision in your mind to set the Sabbath apart as a day of spiritual rejuvenation and a day of rest and fellowship, friendship, and communion with your own family and with God?

* * * * *

"Dear Father, thank You for moving us beyond ceremonies and regulations. Thank You that we don't have to earn a place at Your side. Thank You for giving us a place close to You. Thank You for creating it in the Sabbath. Please enable us to grasp what resting in Christ really means. Help us to be able to truly stop, truly reflect, and truly accept what Christ has accomplished for us. Help us to live in grace. We pray in Your name. Amen."

A Space Big Enough

Do you ever wonder about how your life fits together? Do you ever wonder whether the things that are most important get the most space? Do they get the most time? Or is it the small, urgent things that fill up your days?

Today, we'll discover how to get space for what matters most.

A while back, I came across an interesting article from a special insert in the *Los Angeles Times*. Syndicated columnist Arianna Huffington was writing about "multitasking." That's a phrase that refers to working on several tasks simultaneously. It's often used with computers or organizations. But Arianna was looking at multitasking in everyday life, in our personal lives.

More and more we find ourselves trying to do two or three things at once. We try to open our mail and talk to the kids at the same time. We try to cook supper, catch the evening news, and plan tomorrow's schedule at the same time. We're checking our email on the way out the door, or grabbing a bite on the run, or phoning our spouse on the freeway.

Some people even get hooked on multitasking. As Arianna writes: "Some of my friends feel alive only when they're living life on the brink, dealing with half a dozen crises, wallowing in the drama of it all, and having to drug themselves to sleep" (*Olam,* Winter 2000, p. 9).

In contrast to all this, Arianna recalled the way her mother lived. Mrs. Huffington's world was more timeless. She didn't suffer from the tyranny of the urgent. There were no impersonal encounters at the farmer's market where she shopped. She talked to everyone. A trip to the market might happily fill half a day. This woman took time to appreciate colors and textures, to notice how lovely the rosemary looked next to the lavender.

Arianna recalls: "Going through the market with her was like walking through the Louvre with an art connoisseur—except that you could touch and smell these still lifes."

Mrs. Huffington believed that we miss life, we miss its gifts, unless we give ourselves 100 percent to a task, a relationship, a moment.

After her mother died, Arianna longed to recover some of the timelessness of her world. And she realized that she could—through a gift that God had given to the world, the gift of the Sabbath.

In this special day of rest she could move the important things to the center of life and escape the tyranny of the urgent. It was a space in which she could nurture her soul. The Sabbath enabled Arianna to engage in what she called her "new, new thing— single tasking."

A space in which to focus on what's most important—that's something wonderful to have in our world today. That's one reason there's been a renewed interest in the Sabbath. "Olam," the *Los Angeles Times* special magazine, is just one example. More and more, popular books are being written on the subject. And many Christians are rediscovering the value of God's day of rest.

We're living in a world that increasingly drowns out the still, small voice of God.

We are living in a world where the urgent pushes aside the important. Things don't fit together as they should. That's why so many individuals are taking another look at the Sabbath.

I'd like to tell you why I, as a Christian, have come to appreciate this special day of rest—because God fills up the space that we give Him. This is probably the biggest reason the Sabbath is important to me. That's an important principle. God fills up the space that we give Him. If we only give Him a little space, we're going to have a very little God.

Now, think about this principle in terms of our everyday chores and responsibilities. It's often said that a task fills up the time we give to it. In other words, if we have all day to get a certain thing done, it'll probably take all day.

Sometimes that's a good thing. Jane decided to do something she'd been putting off for a long time—

getting her family photographs organized. She had been trying to get them all into albums during the few minutes of spare time she had—here and there. It just never happened.

But one Sunday, she decided to set aside a couple of hours for the project. She laid out the pictures in chronological order. She labeled them and grouped them according to special events in her family's life. She began writing down anecdotes about family milestones, things she'd almost forgotten. Old stories came vividly back to Jane's mind. And Jane ended up spending the entire day on the photo albums. It wasn't just a little chore to get through anymore. It was an adventure in her family's legacy. It was a wonderful day she'd never forget.

Tasks fill up the time we give them. Sometimes they do that in wonderful ways.

Well, that's even truer of God. He fills up the space we give Him. He can fill us with wonderful pictures of who He is. He can become a wonderful legacy in our lives. But we have to give God space.

Too often today, God occupies pretty cramped quarters in our lives. We confine Him to the corners—when we have a few minutes to spare. We permit Him the space we have left over. We give Him some thought on special holidays or send up a desperate prayer during emergencies. Our days are filled up with so many other things, so many other urgent things here on earth. It's hard to squeeze in much time for our Father in heaven.

But what happens when God gets pushed into the corners? Our God gets smaller and smaller. His voice gets weaker and weaker. He seems more and more distant. And pretty soon, He's just a tiny figure somewhere out there, a figure we occasionally give a nod to.

God has shrunk considerably for most people in our world today. He's a condensed version of the Lord our forefathers worshipped. The writers of the Bible, in fact, would hardly recognize the God of today.

Listen to how the psalmist celebrated the Lord of heaven and earth. The Hebrews were surrounded by cultures that had miniature gods, idols that could be manipulated. But the Hebrews lifted up a far grander God, a far greater God. Listen to the grandeur in these verses from Psalm 47: "Shout to God with the voice of triumph! For the Lord Most High is awesome; He is a great King over all the earth. . . . God reigns over the nations; God sits on His holy throne" (Psalm 47:1, 2, 8).

The God of the Bible isn't confined to any corners. The psalmist looks up to Him in awe, knowing that nothing can contain Him, not even the glorious temple in Jerusalem. He reigns over all the nations.

This kind of God brings a special kind of comfort to human beings in the world, a world in which it's easy to feel pretty insignificant—and sometimes very lost.

Listen to these verses from Psalm 139: "If I ascend into heaven, You are there; if I make my bed in hell, behold, You are there. If I take the wings of the morning, and dwell in the uttermost parts of the sea, even there Your hand shall lead me, and Your right hand shall hold me" (Ps. 139:8-10).

The psalmist celebrated a big God, a God big enough to take in the farthest wanderings, a God big enough to hold us in His arms—wherever we go.

Why did the Hebrews have such a firm hold on a grander God—in a world of miniature gods? One important reason is that they gave God room. They gave Him space to fill up. In fact, every week they set aside an entire day for Him to fill—the Sabbath. And they believed that the Sabbath was a memorial to the Creator God, this huge God of the universe. And they remembered to keep the Sabbath holy.

Listen to how the prophet Ezekiel reminded them of the importance of this special day of rest. He brings this message from God: "I am the Lord your God: Walk in My statutes, keep My judgments, and do them; hallow My Sabbaths, and they will be a sign between Me and you, that you may know that I am the Lord your God" (Ezek. 20:19, 20).

The Sabbath served as a sign linking God and His people. It enabled them to know this one-and-only God. It enabled them to keep their focus on the Lord of heaven and earth. It was a space set aside each week that God filled up. And because He filled it up, the world was given a wonderful picture of a God who is big enough, a God who is far grander than any idol.

God fills up the space we give Him. And if we give Him each Sabbath, He'll fill it up with wonderful blessings. And we need very much to give Him space today. We need to rediscover the grander God of our forefathers and mothers.

Let me tell you about the kind of God who emerges when He has enough room in our lives. Let me tell you just what it means to have a bigger God in your life.

First of all, a big God is Someone who can take care of our needs. A big God is a great Provider. It's ironic that we often lose sight of that precisely because we're so busy trying to provide for ourselves. We all need to work, of course. But often, the struggle to "get ahead" takes over our lives. It would help if we gave God space to become a very present provider. That would make us much more productive in the long run.

Read how the psalmist expresses his faith: "You open Your hand and satisfy the desire of every living thing" (Ps. 145:16).

The writers of Scripture picture a God who clothes the fields with grain and refreshes the earth with dew and rain. They were people who could look at the lilies of the field and trust in their great Provider. Their God was big enough.

And He was big enough to make provision even in the most trying of circumstances. They looked back on a God who had provided for the children of Israel in the wilderness. Psalm 114 says: "Tremble, O earth, at the presence of the Lord . . . who turned the rock into a pool of water, the flint into a fountain of waters" (Ps. 114:7, 8).

Moses once struck a rock, at God's command, and a spring gushed out. Thirsty people were satisfied.

The Hebrews celebrated an awesome God, whose presence could make the whole earth tremble.

Do you know what? If we give God enough space, He'll fill the whole world. He'll fill our world as our great Provider.

I'd like to give you an opportunity to give God some space in your life. Why not start practicing how to do it right now, as you're reading this chapter?

So please, get comfortable and take a few deep breaths. Enjoy the music and the images that follow. Think about the words of Scripture. And let God fill up this space you're giving Him. Let Him fill up your whole world.

Give God enough space, and He'll fill the earth; He'll fill it as the great Provider. That's one great truth that emerges.

Let me show you another one. Here's something else we realize about God when He becomes big enough.

He not only fills the whole earth; He fills the heavens above us. He not only expands horizontally; He expands vertically. In other words, God expands as a moral force in our lives, as a source of inspiration.

When we confine God to the corners of our lives, His voice grows small. We don't sense His moral authority. A downsized voice of conscience is something we can easily ignore.

The Hebrews caught a startling sense of God's moral voice when He thundered above Mount Sinai amid lightning and fire and smoke. God was filling the heavens. And that shook them up. But God's law would become something that defined them as a people for generations to come.

We need a God who is big enough to take us to a higher place, to inspire us to reach higher ground. We need the kind of God prophets such as Isaiah pictured.

Listen to these words from the Lord recorded in Isaiah: "For as the heavens are higher than the earth, so are My ways higher than your ways, and My thoughts than your thoughts" (Isa. 55:9).

Too often, we confine God to *our* ideas, *our* sentiments, *our* attitudes. God needs more room than that. He's grander than anything we can imagine. His truths are big enough to fill the heavens.

Take some time right now to absorb that fact. Meditate on the words and images that follow—and give God space. Let Him grow bigger in your mind and heart. Let Him fill up the heavens. If you give God enough space, He'll fill up the heavens as your great Inspiration. He'll become a moral force in your life.

How big is your God today? Does He fill up the heavens and the earth? Is He a great Provider? Is He a great Inspiration?

Perhaps you've allowed Him to occupy a smaller and smaller space in your life. Perhaps He's been slipping into the corners.

It's time to give God the room He deserves. God fills up the space that we give Him.

It's time to give God serious time in our lives.

And I'd like to suggest the Sabbath day of rest as a great way to start. Devote the Sabbath to God each week and see what happens. Give Him the Sabbath time. Don't fill it up with anything else. Let God fill it. Give Him room to work. I think you'll be amazed at how much bigger and grander God becomes. I think you'll see Him in new ways, and I think you'll begin to see Him fill up the heavens and the earth in your life.

This very week, why not say, "God, there have been so many things in my stress-filled, hectic, frenzied life that seem to squeeze You out. But God, I want to step back. I want to take a deep breath. I want You to fill up my heart. I want You to fill up my mind. I want You to fill up my life. And Lord, I'm going to allow my mind to go back to Creation, back to the day You created the world. And, Lord, I am going to allow you to have that seventh day of the week, the Sabbath, as a special time to fill my life." Would you like to make that commitment now?

* * * * *

"Dear Father, please forgive us for reducing You to our size. Please forgive us for pushing You into the corners. We'd like to start giving You space right now. We'd like to give You one day a week, the Sabbath day, so You can fill it up, so that we can be Your people every day of the week. Give us the strength, the power each week to dedicate the Sabbath to You. And help us make that a regular practice. Help us to carry out this commitment. We ask this in the name of Jesus Christ, our Lord and Savior. Amen."

The Safest Place on Earth

You can't find it in Jerusalem, a city full of religious holy places, an ancient city built on the promise of *shalom,* peace. Today, Jerusalem can offer no real place of safety.

You can't find it in the classic modern metropolis, in the impressive skyscrapers of New York. An office in the richest of trading firms doesn't guarantee you'll be safe.

You can't find it in elegant European capitals such as Rome or Paris. The threat of terror can reach into the heart of those cities as well.

You can't even find it when you get away from it all. Go as far into nature as you will—and danger can still sweep over you.

Today, more than ever, human beings are looking for a place of safety, something we can always count on, a spot of peace in a very jittery world. And you are about to discover a unique place in time that can become for each one of us—the safest place on earth.

In the world of the twenty-first century, more and more people find themselves reaching back for roots. But it isn't really just ethnic roots that we're searching for today. It's something more basic, it's bigger than that. People want to find something they are connected to that won't change, that won't go up in smoke, that won't collapse. People are looking for roots that go down into bedrock.

And in this chapter, I'd like to share with you something God created that exactly fits what we're longing for today. I'd like to show you how it has served as a place of safety through generations, through centuries. We're going to trace it through the whole Bible, from Genesis to Revelation. And we're going to see how this special divine gift can give us roots, roots in the eternal.

I'm excited about this study. So sit back and get ready to take in a big picture that can change your life—in a very jittery world.

We'll start at the very beginning—in Genesis. Did you know that at Creation, God actually gave us two important institutions? The first was marriage. Our Creator united Adam and Eve as one flesh.

The second is described in Genesis: "Then God blessed the seventh day and sanctified it, because in it He rested from all His work which God had created and made" (Gen. 2:3).

At the end of the six days of Creation week, God sanctified the seventh day. He made it holy in a special sense. It was set apart from the rest of the week. It was set apart as a day of rest, an island in time where human beings could escape the everyday demands of earning a living.

That's the first fact the Bible presents us about the Sabbath—it's an island in time, cut off from the ordinary.

Now, we move on to the book of Exodus. The children of Israel are delivered from Egypt and enter into a covenant with God. They're called to share the good news about the one God of heaven with the world. And they are given His essential moral principles—the Ten Commandments. The fourth one explains what the Sabbath means. It's found in Exodus, chapter 20: "Remember the Sabbath day, to keep it holy. . . . For in six days the Lord made the heavens and the earth, the sea, and all that is in them, and rested the seventh day. Therefore the Lord blessed the Sabbath day and hallowed it" (Exod. 20:8, 11).

This fourth commandment points us back to our origin as children of God. God wants us to remember the Sabbath day. Why? Because it connects us to Him as our Creator. It tells us where our roots lie.

The Sabbath is a memorial in time that declares we're not just material specks in a mechanical universe. We didn't just evolve out of the ooze by an incredible series of accidents. No, we come from the hand of an all-powerful, all-wise, eternal God. We're created in His image. He cares for us as His children.

That fact was emphasized during Israel's wandering through the wilderness. Manna fell from heaven in that hostile desert; it fell six days out of seven.

Exodus, chapter 16, tells us that God made it a point to send twice as much manna on Friday so the Israelites wouldn't have to go out and gather it on Saturday, the seventh day. The manna stayed fresh all through the Sabbath.

God was creating a place of safety and security for His people. Enter into Sabbath rest, and your needs will be cared for. That was the message the children of Israel experienced, week after week.

The Sabbath is God's way of letting us experience something of His constancy, His faithfulness. Listen to the Creator Himself expanding on the fourth commandment in Exodus 31:13: "Surely My Sabbaths you shall keep, for it is a sign between Me and you throughout your generations, that you may know that I am the Lord who sanctifies you."

The Sabbath is a sign that continues through generation after generation. It points generation after generation toward the Lord who sanctifies us. Notice that word *sanctify*. Just as God sanctified the seventh day, He can sanctify each one of us; He can set us apart for a special purpose.

And we can experience that regularly when we observe the seventh day as a day of rest, a day to stop our usual routine, a day to spend quality time with family and with God. Our Creator promises that the special blessing available on the day He made holy will continue from generation to generation, from century to century.

Now, let's move on in the Bible to the book of Deuteronomy. Here, Moses looks back on the beginnings of the nation of Israel and talks about what it means to connect with the God of heaven as a people. Listen to how he amplifies the meaning of the Sabbath. He restates the fourth commandment in this way: "And remember that you were a slave in the land of Egypt, and that the Lord your God brought you out from there by a mighty hand and by an outstretched arm; therefore the Lord your God commanded you to keep the Sabbath day" (Deut. 5:15).

The Sabbath, we find here, is also a memorial of God's deliverance as well as a memorial of His creative power. The Hebrews were slaves in Egypt. They had no way to protect themselves. They were at the mercy of their masters' whims. But God stretched out His arm. God rescued them from oppression. God took them safely through the perils of the desert. God established them in the Promised Land, flowing with milk and honey.

"So," God says, "keep the Sabbath. Each week stop and remember. Each week remember that you have a place of safety because I am a great Deliverer." The Sabbath ties us to the God whose hand is stretched out to help us in any and every situation.

In order to enter that island in time, that place of safety, we simply need to keep the Sabbath holy, to set it apart, to give God space in which to come close to us.

OK, let's move on in the story. After the Israelites settled in Canaan, there was the long period of the monarchy, the story told in Kings and Chronicles. In this period, the big struggle was between idols and the living God, between heathen rites and true worship.

This struggle stands out in the whole history of religion. The religions of the world have ascribed holiness to many things. They have considered many places to be holy. But in the Bible, we find the unique idea of holiness in time. God created a holy setting where we could be specially blessed. But He didn't restrict it to a certain location. We don't have to make long pilgrimages to arrive at God's holy place.

No, He has inserted His holy setting in time, equally accessible to everyone. It's a place in time we can all enter each week. And it's something that will always be there—in a world of constant change and confusion.

And the Old Testament prophets kept calling the people back to God the Creator, to God the Lawgiver, to God the Deliverer.

Here's something they emphasized. Let's look at Jeremiah, chapter 17. Here, Jeremiah delivers a message from God, urging His people to observe the Sabbath carefully: "Take heed to yourselves, and bear no burden on the Sabbath day, nor bring it in by the gates of Jerusalem . . . nor do any work, but hallow the Sabbath day, as I commanded your fathers" (Jer. 17:21, 22).

Jeremiah is conveying a message about a danger we all face. Constant work can squeeze out spirituality. The pursuit of money can eat up all our time. It happened back then in Jerusalem. It happens today.

And God is saying, "Don't neglect the Sabbath. Don't let the pursuit of material security overwhelm the pursuit of the kind of security that matters most."

The prophet Isaiah takes up this same theme. In chapter 58 he's asking his people to rebuild their faith. He's calling them back to spiritual values. And this is what he says: "You shall raise up the foundations of many generations; and you shall be called the Repairer of the Breach, the Restorer of Streets to Dwell In. If you turn away your foot from the Sabbath, from doing your pleasure on My holy day, and call the Sabbath a delight, the holy day of the Lord honorable . . . I will cause you to ride on the high hills of the earth" (Isa. 58:12-14).

Note that those who rebuild the faith are called "Repairers of the Breach." Obviously there was a breach in the protective wall that surrounded God's people. That boundary had been broken down. And Isaiah's call to repair the breach is associated with a call to restore the Sabbath, to make it a delight again, to make it honorable again.

Why? Because the Sabbath is a place of safety. It's part of that protective wall, part of God's circle of care around us. It's a special way for us to experience that caring presence each week.

And what's more, God promises that if we honor the Sabbath, He will cause us to "ride on the high hills of the earth." That's not a picture of people who are afraid. That's not a picture of people hunkering down waiting for the next calamity to strike. That's a picture of people who are confident and safe—in an unsafe world. They're riding high because they've found the safest place on earth. And that place was always there, through all the ups and downs of Israel's history.

It even followed them through exile in the land of Babylon, and back again. The books of Ezra and Nehemiah tell us the story of the Hebrews who came back home. They managed to rebuild their temple, reestablish their city, and renew their covenant with God.

In Nehemiah, chapter 13, we find one important element of that renewal. Governor Nehemiah had to confront some Hebrew nobles who were conducting business as usual on the seventh day: "What evil thing is this that you do, by which you profane the Sabbath day? Did not your fathers do thus, and did not our God bring all this disaster on us and on this city? Yet you bring added wrath on Israel by profaning the Sabbath" (Neh. 13:17, 18).

What is Nehemiah saying here? He's saying that knowingly profaning the Sabbath takes people out of a place of safety. The reason Israel collapsed, the reason that nation was overrun by a Babylonian army, was that they'd forgotten about God the Creator, the great Deliverer. They'd stopped giving Him time. They'd stopped giving Him space. And so they ended up in a very dangerous place. They ended up as captives in a heathen land.

So, Nehemiah wanted them to honor God, by honoring the Sabbath. That's how they could build a place of security once again. That's how they could find an island of safety in a hostile world. That's how they could stay connected with something eternal.

The story of the Sabbath sweeps through the Bible like a great river. It makes the themes of Creation, Redemption, and covenant flow together. It invites us to experience eternity in the present.

But now let's move on to the New Testament. What about Jesus? How did He relate to the Sabbath?

Well, as a matter of fact, one of the things Jesus was most noted for in His day was His stand on Sabbath observance. It was very controversial. He got into continual conflict with the Pharisees on this issue. Jesus wanted to fill the Sabbath with joy and blessings. The Pharisees were filling it with regulations.

One Sabbath day, Jesus was teaching in the synagogue as was His custom. A woman who had been crippled for many years was brought in, bent nearly double. Jesus approached the woman and placed His hands on her. Immediately, she straightened up and began praising God.

Instead of joining in these thankful praises, the Pharisees became indignant. Jesus had healed someone. Healing was work; it was labor. There were six days for that. Why heal on the seventh?

Jesus was ready with an answer. He cried out, "Does not each one of you on the Sabbath loose his ox or his donkey from the stall, and lead it away to water it? So ought not this woman, being a daughter of Abraham, whom Satan has bound—think of it—for eighteen years, be loosed from this bond on the Sabbath?" (Luke 13:15, 16).

Jesus' opponents were humiliated. Their pettiness was exposed. What kind of religion would permit an animal to be watered, but prevent the relief of human suffering?

For Jesus, the Sabbath was a time for healing. It was a time for laying down burdens, not taking them up. It was a time when people could find relief and rest. It was a place of safety. Of course, the crippled and lame and blind were welcome inside its shelter!

Jesus' attitude toward the Sabbath can be summed up in a simple, but profound, statement He made in response to His critics: "The Sabbath was made for man, and not man for the Sabbath. Therefore the Son of Man is also Lord of the Sabbath" (Mark 2:27, 28).

Jesus wanted to free human beings from oppressive religion. He sidestepped ceremony and regulation and showed us a better way into the kingdom. But He did proclaim Himself Lord of the Sabbath. I think that's significant.

To all those who think the Sabbath is part of those old ceremonies, part of the ritual we no longer need, Jesus says, "The Sabbath was made for man." Remember, it was given to us back at the beginning, at Creation.

And to those who would turn the Sabbath experience into a burdensome ritual, Jesus said, "The Sabbath was made for man, and *not* man for the Sabbath." The Sabbath was made to bless us. The Sabbath was made to benefit us. It's not just another religious obligation. It's not just another chore.

The Sabbath continues in the New Testament as the safest place on earth. It continues as a place where we renew our covenant with God, our relationship with Him. That fact comes through in the writings of the apostles, in the letters of the New Testament.

Take a look at Hebrews, chapter four. In this chapter, the writer quotes from the fourth commandment, the one that asks us to keep the seventh day holy. He reminds his readers that "God rested on the seventh day from all His works" (Heb. 4:4). Then, a few verses later, the author writes: "There remains therefore a rest for the people of God. For he who has entered His rest has himself also ceased from his works as God did from His" (Heb. 4:9, 10).

What is this text telling us? The Bible Sabbath, as opposed to the Sabbath of church tradition, is still important for the people of God. It's still useful. And it has a very special meaning for the New Testament believer. The Creator rested from His works on the seventh day, on Saturday of Creation week.

We, too, can rest from our labors. We rest in God's completed work—both of Creation and Redemption. God worked out our salvation by giving up His Son on the cross. That great act of grace and acceptance is finished, completed. We don't have to try to earn it. We don't have to try to pay God back for it. We simply accept it. We rest in grace.

The Sabbath should *never* be a symbol of legalism. It's a beautiful symbol of grace, of resting in the finished work of Jesus Christ.

That's really the most important reason why the Sabbath is the safest place on earth. Nothing can make us more secure than what Christ accomplished for us on the cross. And the Sabbath reminds us to rest in that, to trust in that, each week. It's a practical way of experiencing those arms of love wrapped around us.

Have you discovered that rest? Have you found a place of ultimate safety today?

May I encourage you to begin experiencing God's Sabbath rest each week? This is a wonderful way for you to put down your roots in something unchanging, something eternal. This is your personal connection to God the Creator, to God the Redeemer, to the God who sets you apart.

So, I invite you to make this investment of time each week, to set this day apart each week. I guarantee you will find a great blessing. You will find that this time really does become holy. It really does become something irreplaceable in your life.

* * * * *

"Dear Father, thank You for giving us this island in time, this island of peace and grace called the Sabbath. Please help us to begin experiencing this day as You intended. Please help us to truly give You this time and open our lives to this blessing. Teach us how to make the Sabbath a special, delightful day for ourselves and our families. We ask it in the name of Jesus. Amen."

Whose Flag Will Fly?

Have you ever stopped to wonder that if this world is going to end with a bang—who does the banging? Does anybody win? In other words, what flag will be flying above the ruins? Does God have a flag? Can we make sure we're giving Him our allegiance—in a world filled with so many competing claims for the one-and-only truth?

The stakes are higher today. The voices are louder. The clash of cultures and religions is more intense. We thought we'd left "holy wars" behind in the Middle Ages. They're back with a vengeance.

There are people out there quite willing to bring your world crashing down if they can't have the world their way. They're willing to go up in smoke to take others down with them. And they proclaim a fierce loyalty to their God, to their faith. They passionately believe that their flag will be the one standing in the end.

How do we know what will remain standing in a time such as this? How do we know what really expresses allegiance to God? How do we know what issue will divide humanity in the end time?

I'd like to try to answer those questions in this chapter. I think the Bible gives us some important clues, and they are clues that cut across the dividing lines of culture and religion.

One of the most enlightening examples of allegiance comes to us from the Old Testament book of Daniel. There's a conflict documented there that speaks powerfully to our conflicts today.

The third chapter of Daniel presents us with a remarkable scene on the Plain of Dura near ancient Babylon. An enormous gold statue of King Nebuchadnezzar had been set up. Thousands of representatives from his empire had been invited to pay homage to it in a splendid ceremony. This king was making a statement. He was saying, "I will be left standing when other kings and empires have fallen." Babylon, he was saying, would last forever.

But just as the vast assembly bowed to the ground toward the image, something interrupted the proceedings. Three young men remained sanding. They were three young Jewish princes, Shadrach, Meshach, and Abednego. They'd been brought as captives to Babylon and were being trained to help govern its great empire.

And now, they stuck out like sore thumbs. Babylonian officials quickly brought Nebuchadnezzar the news. This wasn't just a diplomatic error. This was treason. It was treason because the king's herald had made an announcement a few moments before, in a loud voice that rang over the plain.

His words are recorded in Daniel: "To you it is commanded, O peoples, nations, and languages, that at the time you hear the sound of the horn . . . you shall fall down and worship the gold image that King Nebuchadnezzar has set up; and whoever does not fall down and worship shall be cast immediately into the midst of a burning fiery furnace" (Dan. 3:4-6).

The king had made this act of worship a test of loyalty. Nebuchadnezzar wanted total allegiance. Well, that put the three Hebrews in a terrible bind. They'd been taught since childhood that there was only one Being worthy of worship. Bowing down to an idol was a betrayal of their faith. And yet, if they didn't bow down, they'd be burned to death!

Pretty tough choice! What would you do in a situation like that? How important are these gestures of allegiance? That's a vital question for us today when suicide bombers are willing to blow up themselves and innocent bystanders to declare their allegiance to a cause.

Interestingly enough, Nebuchadnezzar's decree has a striking parallel in the Bible. It's echoed by a decree found in the book of Revelation. Revelation, chapter 13, talks about a challenge God's people will face at the end of time. The antichrist sets up an image to his representative, the beast:

> He was granted power to give breath to the image of the beast, that the image of the beast should both speak and cause as many as would not worship the image of the beast to be killed.

And he causes all, both small and great, rich
and poor, free and slave, to receive a mark on
their right hand or on their foreheads, and
that no one may buy or sell except one who
has the mark or the name of the beast, or the
number of his name (Rev. 13:15-17).

This decree will test our allegiance in the end times.
Now, notice the parallels between Nebuchadnezzar's
decree and the decree in Revelation:

- In both, a world leader attempts to compel worship to an image.
- In both, there is something that contradicts God's specific commandment to worship Him alone.
- In both, all who do not submit are condemned to death.

Whom are we going to bow down to? That's the
ultimate question. At some point, believers are going to be confronted by a great power, a religious
and political power, that demands our ultimate allegiance. And the issue is worship. That's the flag.
There's good worship and bad worship. There's true
worship and false worship. Just because people are
raising their voices in the name of God doesn't mean
they have the right kind of allegiance. They could
be waving assault rifles right along with their
praises.

You know, the theme of worship runs all through
the book of Revelation:

- In Revelation 4, living creatures bow before the throne of God, surrounded by an emerald rainbow. They declare day and night, "Holy, holy, holy, Lord God Almighty" (verse 8).
- In Revelation 5, thousands and thousands of angels lift up their voices: "Worthy is the Lamb who was slain" (verse 12).
- In Revelation 7, a great multitude from every nation on earth lifts up palm branches before the God of their salvation (see verses 9, 10).

Scenes like this are repeated until we come to joyous worship in the New Jerusalem as the nations walk in God's light. But let's look at how this theme comes into sharp focus in the very heart of the book. Revelation 12 and 13 introduce us to symbolic creatures who represent evil forces in the world—the beast, the dragon, and the false prophet. They are trying to get everyone to bow down to that image of the beast.

And then, in Revelation 14, we find God's dramatic response to this great challenge, His response to false worship. It is, in fact, the Almighty's final message of warning to the world. It's given by three angels flying in the sky who have an eternal gospel to proclaim. This is what they say: "Fear God and give glory to Him, for the hour of His judgment has come; and worship Him who made heaven and earth, the sea and springs of water" (Rev. 14:7).

Who is it that we are called to worship? The Creator of heaven and earth, the One who breathes life into every creature. Only our Creator has the right to judge us; we are responsible to Him and Him alone.

True worship focuses on the God who stands above us as Creator and Judge. It's to Him that we need to give our allegiance.

The angels of Revelation 14 go on to warn about the terrible fate of those who worship the beast: "If anyone worships the beast and his image . . . he himself shall also drink of the wine of the wrath of God" (Rev. 14:9, 10).

Notice that here we see the counterpoint to the first angel's message. We are *not* to worship the beast; we *are* to worship the Creator. These two choices stand in opposition. The one calls us into a false allegiance to something man-made. The other calls us to give God glory, to worship Him as Creator.

Worshiping the beast is deadly. So how do we stand against it when pressured to conform? How do we keep from worshiping its image? By fixing an unconditional faith on our Creator. His authority must supersede all others. Give Him glory.

May I give you a very practical suggestion? There is actually a way for you to express your unconditional allegiance to the Creator regularly, every week. It's found in the fourth commandment. This is something many Christians have overlooked:

Remember the Sabbath day, to keep it holy. Six days you shall labor and do all your work, but the seventh day is the Sabbath of the Lord your God. . . . For in six days the Lord made

the heavens and the earth, the sea, and all
that is in them, and rested the seventh day.
Therefore the Lord blessed the Sabbath day
and hallowed it (Exod. 20:8-11).

Why are we urged to observe the seventh day, Saturday? Because it's a memorial of Creation. It ties us
to our Creator. It's a rest in God's finished work. The
fourth commandment asks us to remember the One
who made the heavens and the earth.

The Sabbath, then, is a symbol of our love and loyalty to our Creator. May I suggest that this can be a
wonderful way to protect ourselves from the wrong kind
of allegiance? Think again of that decree of the antichrist
in Revelation, the decree that demands everyone bow
down to the image of the beast—on pain of death.

I believe that a fiery trial is coming to our world, a
time of trouble greater than any that we've experienced in history. God's followers are going to be
brought to a crisis over the issue of the commandments of God, over tyranny, over enforced worship.

So we need to make sure we're worshiping the right
God in the right way. That's the issue. Those three
young Hebrews standing on the Plain of Dura un-
derstood that well. Let's return to their story.

King Nebuchadnezzar was outraged, of course, that
anyone would interrupt his moment of glory. He had
the three brought before him. He pointed to the blaz-
ing furnaces. He asked, very pointedly, "Who is the
god who will deliver you from my hands?" (Dan. 3:15).

The answer these Hebrew youth gave is justly famous. Fearlessly, they replied to the king, "O Nebuchadnezzar . . . our God whom we serve is able to deliver us from the burning fiery furnace. . . . But if not, let it be known to you, O king, that we do not serve your gods, nor will we worship the gold image which you have set up" (Dan. 3:16-18).

These men answered the proud king's challenge without hesitation. They did so by testifying of their faith in the God of heaven and earth. They were committed to worshiping Him alone, even if He did not deliver them from death.

And what was the result? Well, an enraged Nebuchadnezzar had his furnace fired up to the maximum. Then he had the Hebrews thrown into the flames! Apparently their God wasn't going to save them.

But He did. In fact, He made a wonderful appearance, right in the midst of that fiery furnace. Nebuchadnezzar was astonished to observe another figure in the furnace, standing beside the three men he had thrown into the fire. He cried out, "I see four men loose, walking in the midst of the fire; and they are not hurt, and the form of the fourth is like the Son of God" (Dan. 3:25).

Three men had been thrown in. But four were alive and well in that furnace! Shadrach, Meshach, and Abednego were walking in the flames with the Son of God at their side!

You know, the book of Daniel teaches us something important—the final crisis outlined in the book of Revelation need not terrify us. It can be an opportunity for us to see our Lord, very close and very powerful. These young Hebrews had their eyes fixed on a great God. And in their hour of trial, they found that a great God had come to be with them. That's what an unconditional faith, a committed faith, can do for us. It will bring God close in the worst of times.

Let me tell you about a remarkable man who exhibited this kind of faith. His story comes to us through the great evangelist of India—Sundhar Singh. In one of his many journeys through the Himalayas, he discovered a Tibetan preacher whom the people treated with great reverence. This man could proclaim Christ without fear of reprisal, even though other preachers were violently persecuted. This is why.

At one time, he'd served as secretary to a lama. But a visiting Christian from the Punjab told him about the gospel. Eventually, he declared himself a follower of Jesus. The first who heard about it was his own master, the Buddhist lama, who happened to be an ignorant fanatic.

Within a few days, the preacher was sentenced to death. Strong men bound a wet yak skin around him and sewed it up tight. They left him in front of the lamasery walls—in the scorching sunshine. There, the contracting skin would crush him to death.

The preacher, however, didn't die. So they thrust red-hot skewers through the yak skin into his body. Later they tore off the skin and dragged the man through the streets to a refuse dump outside of town. After further abuse, the preacher was dropped on a dunghill. His body showed no signs of life. The crowds left. The vultures gathered.

But this mutilated victim had not died. Somehow, he managed to crawl away and recover. And then, instead of fleeing for his life, he marched right back into the village and began preaching about Christ. He could still testify about his faith. He could speak of a great God who had come close. And now, people listened in awe.

Those three Hebrews in the fiery furnace made quite an impression too. King Nebuchadnezzar rushed up to the edge of the furnace and called to them to come out. As they emerged, a large crowd gathered around. They noticed that their hair wasn't even singed! Their clothes didn't even smell of smoke!

Ultimately, that fiery trial the Hebrews went through burned only one thing—the ropes that bound them. It freed them from their bonds. Shadrach, Meshach, and Abednego came out of the furnace as conquerors.

For the first time, King Nebuchadnezzar realized that there might be a God in heaven far bigger than he could ever be. He acknowledged that these three Hebrews were "servants of the Most High God." Up to this point, the king had tried to be the most high himself, with his massive golden statue.

But now, he made a remarkable confession. We find it in Daniel, chapter three: "Blessed be the God of Shadrach, Meshach, and Abed-Nego, who sent His Angel and delivered His servants who trusted in Him, and they have frustrated the king's word, and yielded their bodies, that they should not serve nor worship any god except their own God!" (Dan. 3:28).

Nebuchadnezzar's rage had turned to reverence. He realized that another kind of allegiance was important. He realized that he needed to worship the right God in the right way. He needed to bow before the God who comes close in times of trouble.

That's the God who deserves our allegiance today.

My friend, history is headed toward a climax. Two kinds of allegiance are battling for supremacy on this planet, two kinds of worship. We will either worship the Creator or we will worship something man-made. We will either worship the Lord of heaven and earth, or we will worship someone who promises us heaven on earth. We will either place our faith in the invisible, Holy God, or we will be captured by the dazzle of an image. We'll either stand for His truth, or we will be swept up by the crowd.

In small ways and in big ways, the battle lines are being drawn. Hate is disguised as religious fervor. Fanatical allegiance claims to be the one true faith. "My side," "my tradition," replaces the law of God. Battle lines are being drawn right now between the empire of Satan and the empire of Christ. And the bad guys don't always wear white hats. We can't just condemn this or that group or write off this or that culture.

As Jesus said, the wheat and the weeds are growing close together. The good and the bad are intertwined. *But* the dividing line is not blurred. It runs right through each individual heart. There's a clear distinction. Where's our allegiance? Do we bow before Someone greater and grander than us? Or do we bow before an image we make—an image that suits our prejudice, our tradition, our private truth?

I want to stand with those three brave Hebrews on the Plain of Dura. I want to stand with them now. I want to stand with them in the time of the end. And I believe their kind of faith is available to each and every one of us, a faith that will stand tall when times get rough. It's really a matter of perspective. What do we choose to place at the center of our lives? Who gets first place? Whose truth gets top priority?

Please make sure you remember the Creator of heaven and earth. Take time to remember. Take time to worship. Take time now before the clash of allegiances makes it too late.

The Creator—the Lord—the Judge—the Lawgiver—the Redeemer—the One who loves us to the uttermost—He alone deserves our worship. Please don't fall for any other image. Please don't fall for any counterfeit vision. I promise you won't ever bow before the wrong thing, if you're already worshiping the right God. I promise you will stand, because He stands with you; He walks with you—even in the fire.

* * * * *

"Father, we acknowledge You as our Creator and as our Redeemer. Thank You that, no matter how overwhelming the conflict might seem, You are able to deliver. We know that times are coming when our allegiance will be tested. But we know that You can make us loyal and courageous and true. We place our trust in You as that kind of God. Teach us to develop that trust in the midst of conflicts day by day. Come close to us in the fire. In Jesus' name, Amen."